Funny You Should Mention It

FUNNY YOU SHO

A Collection o

Selected by Patricia Skalka

HALLMARK EDITIONS

JLD MENTION IT

Classic Humor

Illustrated by Rosalyn Schanzer

FUNNY YOU SHOULD MENTION IT

LOVE

W. C. FIELDS

Can a man love both whiskey and dogs? Certainly. A man can have many loves. . . . He can love whiskey, dogs, cigars, horses and his secretary, to mention only a few. . . .

ROBERT W. CHAMBERS

All the world may not love a lover but all the world watches him.

H. L. MENCKEN

Love is the delusion that one woman differs from another.

CAROLYN WELLS

He who loves and runs away may live to love another day.

RING LARDNER

He gave her a look you could have poured on a waffle.

MARRIAGE

JOHN BARRYMORE

Q. If I refuse to marry you will you really commit suicide?

A. That has been my customary procedure.

W. C. FIELDS

No man is boss in his own home, but he can make up for it, he thinks, by making a dog play dead. . . .

FRED ALLEN

There is no other news except that our oil stove exploded yesterday and blew your father and me out into the back yard. It is the first time we have been out together for twenty years.

FIORELLO H. LAGUARDIA

I lost a good secretary and found a lousy cook.

CHARLIE CHAN

Maybe some people on sea of matrimony wish they had missed boat.

WOMEN

ARTURO TOSCANINI

I kissed my first woman and smoked my first cigarette on the same day; I have never had time for tobacco since.

ED WYNN

Dear Chief:

I am a woman of forty-five years of age. I weigh 187 pounds and have just rented an apartment which is in a court. There are no window shades in the bathroom and I am afraid of taking a bath because my neighbors can see in. My landlord won't buy shades. What shall I do?

Out of Shape

Dear Out of Shape:

If you are really forty-five years of age and if you really weigh 187 pounds, your landlord doesn't have to buy you window shades. You take a bath and your neighbors will buy the shades.

Fire Chief

GERTRUDE BERG

If vanity is the name for women, what should a man be called?

JOHN BARRYMORE

The way to fight a woman is with your hat. Grab it and run.

P. GERALDY

We would give her more consideration, when we judge a woman, if we knew how difficult it is to be a woman.

FANNIE HURST

A woman has to be twice as good as a man to
go half as far.

WALTER WINCHELL

A woman's fondest wish is to be weighed and
found wanting.

CHILDREN

GYPSY ROSE LEE

She's descended of a long line her mother listened to.

W. C. FIELDS

Any man who hates children can't be all bad.

ROBERT BENCHLEY

In America there are two classes of travel—first class and with children.

FRED ALLEN

My father never raised his hand to any one of his children except in self-defense.

CLARENCE DARROW

Whenever I hear people discussing birth control, I always remember that I was the fifth.

HERBERT HOOVER

When word reached President Hoover of the birth of a granddaughter, he remarked, "Thank God, she doesn't have to be confirmed by the Senate."

FAME

ALBEN W. BARKLEY

Two brothers were born to a family in Kentucky. When they grew up one ran off to sea, the other became Vice-President of the United States. Neither was ever heard from again.

H. L. MENCKEN

A celebrity is one who is known to many persons he is glad he doesn't know.

HERBERT HOOVER

In response to a child's request for his autograph, [President] Hoover wrote:

"I was delighted to see that you were not a professional autograph hunter. Once upon a time, one of those asked me for three autographs. I inquired why. He said, 'It takes two of yours to get one of Babe Ruth's'."

ARTHUR G. TRUDEAU

After Wilbur and Orville made their history making flight at Kitty Hawk, N.C., on Dec. 17, 1903, they wrote home about it and added they'd be home in a few days. Their letter reached a Dayton newspaper which headlined the story, "Prominent Local Bicycle Merchants to Be Home for Christmas."

ROBERT BENCHLEY

It took me fifteen years to discover I had no talent for writing, but I couldn't give it up because by that time I was too famous.

WINSTON CHURCHILL

There is the story of the little boy who lived near Chartwell and was taken there by his nanny to see "the greatest man in the whole wide world." W.S.C. had retired for his afternoon nap. While the little boy's nanny had her tea, the child sneaked off to look for his hero and found him reading in bed.

Little boy: Are you the greatest man in the whole wide world?

W.S.C.: Of course I'm the greatest man in the whole wide world. Now buzz off.

FORTUNE

EDDIE CANTOR

We call our rich relatives the kin we love to touch.

ANITA LOOS

Diamonds are a girl's best friend.

ROBERT BENCHLEY

There are several ways in which to apportion the family income, all of them unsatisfactory.

LADY ASTOR

The only thing I like about rich people is their money.

W. C. FIELDS

A rich man is nothing but a poor man with money.

BUSTER KEATON

It has been my observation that being a millionaire alters almost everybody's attitude, and can be as distracting as inheriting a zoo or a harem.

DAMON RUNYON

The race is not always to the swift, nor the battle to the strong—but that's the way to bet.

VICE

ALEXANDER WOOLLCOTT

All the things I like to do are either immoral, illegal, or fattening.

DOROTHY PARKER

Drink, and dance and laugh and lie,
Love, the reeling midnight through,
For tomorrow we shall die!
(But, alas, we never do.)

OSCAR WILDE

He hasn't a single redeeming vice.

JAMES J. WALKER

I never knew a girl who was ruined by a book.

MAE WEST

To err is human, but it feels divine.

VIRTUE

TALLULAH BANKHEAD

It's the good girls who keep diaries; the bad girls never have the time.

WARREN G. HARDING

It's a good thing I wasn't born a girl because I never could say no.

MAE WEST

When I'm good, I'm very, very good, but when I'm bad, I'm better.

RELIGION

H. L. MENCKEN

A church is a place in which gentlemen who have never been to heaven brag about it to persons who will never get there.

FRED ALLEN

The first Sunday I sang in the church choir, two hundred people changed their religion.

BILLY SUNDAY

If there is no hell, a good many preachers are obtaining money under false pretenses.

MARK TWAIN

There are many scapegoats for our sins, but the most popular is providence.

POLITICS

CLIFTON FADIMAN

Born in a log cabin, Ambrose Bierce defied Alger's Law and did not become President.

JOHN GUNTHER

The politician was trying to save both his faces.

WINSTON CHURCHILL

Addressing Lady Nancy Astor, first woman member of Parliament: Nancy, when you entered the House, I felt you had come upon me in my bath and I had nothing to protect me but my sponge.

JOHN NANCE GARNER

Vice-President: a spare tire on the automobile of government.

PROGRESS

GEORGE ADE

"Whom are you?" he said, for he had been to night school.

DOROTHY CANFIELD FISHER

What's the use of inventing a better system as long as there just aren't enough folks with sense to go around.

WILL ROGERS

OGDEN NASH

I think that I shall never see
A billboard lovely as a tree.
Indeed, unless the billboards fall,
I'll never see a tree at all.

DON HEROLD

Methods of locomotion have improved greatly
in recent years, but places to go remain about
the same.

GROUCHO MARX

When I first came to this country, I didn't have
a nickel in my pocket—now I have a nickel in
my pocket.

HARD TIMES

FRED ALLEN

I worked in the (Boston) library for several
years. My salary was 20 cents per hour. For

three hours each night I received 60 cents; when work was over I was hungry. An egg sandwich and a piece of pie cost 10 cents. Another nickel went for carfare home. On the remainder I started to build my fortune. You can appreciate why this wealth is nonexistent today.

EDDIE CANTOR

My throat is cut from ear to ear. I am bleeding profusely in seven other places. There is a knocking in the back of my head, my hands tremble violently, I have sharp shooting pains all over my body, and in addition to all that my general health is none too good.

One of the greatest diagnosticians in America thumped me and probed me all over the premises.

"You are a very sick man!" he said finally. "A very sick man. You are suffering from Montgomery Ward of the liver; General Electric of the stomach; Westinghouse of the brain, and besides you have a severe case of internal combustion. . . ."

INFLATION

W. C. FIELDS

The cost of living has gone up a dollar a quart.

GEORGE BURNS

You know today it costs a young fellow ten dollars to take a girl to lunch. When I was a boy, if you asked your father for ten dollars it meant you were going to get married, and have enough money left over to open a business....

In those days money went a long way. For a dollar you could take a girl to dinner and to a movie and have sodas afterwards. My only problem was to find a girl who had a dollar....

I remember when I was seventeen I had a real big date, and my father gave me a dollar. I told him I'd be home at twelve, but I didn't get in till four in the morning. There was my father, sitting up. He wasn't worried about me, he was waiting for his change....

And when I was a kid, it wasn't always girls. If I had a few nickels saved, I'd go to a ball

24

game. They let you in for fifty cents if you wore long pants, and twenty-five cents if you wore short pants. One day I figured out a way to get in for nothing, but I caught cold before I even left the house.

FASHION

DOROTHY PARKER

Brevity is the soul of lingerie.

LADY ASTOR

What would we say if men changed the length of their trousers every year?

P. G. WODEHOUSE

She looked as if she had been poured into her clothes and had forgotten to say "when."

LIQUOR

WINSTON CHURCHILL

I have taken more out of alcohol than alcohol has taken out of me.

W. C. FIELDS

It was a woman who drove me to drink—and you know, I never even thanked her.

JOE E. LEWIS

I know lots more old drunks than old doctors.

W. C. FIELDS

The advantages of whiskey over dogs are legion. Whiskey does not need to be periodically wormed, it does not need to be fed, it never requires a special kennel, it has no toenails to be clipped or coat to be stripped.... Whiskey sits quietly in its special nook until you want it. True, whiskey has a nasty habit of running out, but then so does a dog.

SOLD AMERICAN

F. W. WOOLWORTH

I am the world's worst salesman; therefore I must make it easy for people to buy.

FRED ALLEN

He is in business for himself. He puts peroxide on sparrows and sells them for canaries.

GERALD BARZAN

I once worked as a salesman and was very independent. I took orders from no one.

GETTING ON

GYPSY ROSE LEE

I have everything I had twenty years ago, only it's all a little bit lower.

ROBERT BENCHLEY

One of the advantages of growing older and putting on weight is that a man can admit to being afraid of certain things, which as a stripling, he had to face without blanching.

FRED ALLEN

The older you get the more people you seem to know in the obituary pages.

FRANKLIN D. ROOSEVELT

The year after Eleanor and I were married, she being twenty-one and I twenty-four, we were at Campobello and had living with us her brother, Hall Roosevelt, aged sixteen. He was rather devoted to a young lady of fourteen who lived in a cottage across the way. One night he came home about 9 P.M. sighing deeply, and turning to Eleanor and me said: "Tell me something—was it customary to hold hands on the porch when you and Eleanor were young?"

DOROTHY CANFIELD FISHER

Being middle-aged is a nice change from being young.

GEORGE GOBEL

For some people life begins at 40, but most of us just spend that year resting up from being 39.

TAKE YOUR MEDICINE

GROUCHO MARX

I have just returned from the desert. My younger daughter and I left Beverly Hills in perfect health. She came back with a sore throat and I came back with a cold. As soon as I regain my health I will be off to some other health resort.

JAMES THURBER

He fell down a great deal during his boyhood because of a trick he had of walking into himself.

JOSH BILLINGS

The best medicine I know for rheumatism is to thank the Lord it ain't the gout.

DIET

WINSTON CHURCHILL

You are afraid to eat your words. There is no
need to be. I have eaten a great many of mine
in my time and on the whole I have found them
a most wholesome diet.

MAE WEST

I never worry about diets. The only carrots that
interest me are the number of carats in a
diamond.

W. C. FIELDS

Once during Prohibition, I was forced to live
for days on nothing but food and water.

FOUR-LEGGED AND OTHER CREATURES

W. C. FIELDS

The whole theory of fox hunting is plainly an excuse to take a drink....What can you do with a fox even if you happen to catch one?

WILL CUPPY

All modern men are descended from wormlike creatures, but it shows more on some people.

ROBERT BENCHLEY

A dog teaches a boy fidelity, perseverance, and to turn around three times before lying down.

CHRISTOPHER MORLEY

Few girls are as well shaped as a good horse.

LOCAL COLOR

JOHN BARRYMORE

America is the country where you buy a lifetime supply of aspirin for one dollar, and use it up in two weeks.

FRED ALLEN

California is a fine place to live in—if you happen to be an orange.

GERTRUDE STEIN

In the United States there is more space where nobody is than where anybody is. This is what makes America what it is.

KATHARINE BRUSH

New Yorkers are nice about giving you street directions; in fact, they seem quite proud of knowing where they are themselves.

W. C. FIELDS

I'd like to see Paris before I die—Philadelphia would do!

RING LARDNER

Beyond those billboards lies New Jersey.

H. L. MENCKEN

As an American, I naturally spend most of my time laughing.

HOLLYWOOD

MACK SENNETT

It was a wet day in Southern California and the pavement in front of Keystone was half an inch deep in mud and water. Chester Conklin spied Mabel (Normand) across the street, wondering how to get across, and made a fancy gesture. He bowed like a headwaiter expecting a fifty-dollar tip, snatched off his coat, and spread it in the mud for Mabel to step on. She stepped, and disappeared into a manhole.

W. C. FIELDS

A Hollywood columnist printed the false news that W. C. Fields was dead. The comedian called the editor in a rage. "I hope you noticed," he screamed, "that your foul newspaper announced this morning that I was dead."

"I did—may I ask where you're calling from?"

GROUCHO MARX

It looks as if Hollywood brides keep the bouquets and throw away the groom.

FRED ALLEN

Hollywood is a place where people from Iowa mistake each other for movie stars.

WILL ROGERS

In Hollywood the woods are full of people that learned to write but evidently can't read; if they could read their stuff, they'd stop writing.

DON'T PLAY IT AGAIN SAM

FRED ALLEN

How can you stop a dead fish from smelling?
Cut off its nose.

CHARLIE MC CARTHY

I hear that the elephants around your place take
aspirin to get rid of W. C. Fields.

GRACIE ALLEN

S. S. Van Dine is silly to spend six or seven
months writing a novel when you can buy one
for two dollars....When I read a book, first I
read the ending, then I read the beginning, and
then I start in the middle and read whichever
way I like best.

39

GEORGE D. PRENTICE

A dentist at work in his vocation always looks down in the mouth.

GEORGE MORAN, CHARLIE MACK

MORAN: What's an alibi?
MACK: An alibi is proving that you was where you was when you wasn't so that you wasn't where you was when you was.

SELF PORTRAITS

W. C. FIELDS

I've been a fragile thing of beauty ever since I was born.

FRED ALLEN

I don't have to look up my family tree, because I know that I'm the sap.

WINSTON CHURCHILL

I both drink and smoke and I'm 200% fit.

MAE WEST

I'm not a little girl from a little town making good in a big town. I'm a big girl from a big town making good in a little town.

TOP THAT

WILL ROGERS

To make money, buy some good stock, hold it until it goes up and then sell it. If it doesn't go up, don't buy it.

CALVIN COOLIDGE

When Coolidge was Vice President, a dinner companion said to him, "You must talk to me, Mr. Coolidge. I made a bet today that I could get more than two words out of you."

"You lose," he said.

BENNETT CERF

When Cornelia Otis Skinner opened in a revival of Shaw's "Candida," he cabled, "Excellent. Greatest." Miss Skinner, overwhelmed, cabled back, "Undeserving such praise." Shaw answered, "I meant the play." Miss Skinner bristled and replied, "So did I."

JOSH BILLINGS

The habits of skunks are phew! but unique.

GROUCHO MARX

If you're insulted, you can leave in a taxi. If that's not fast enough, you can leave in a huff. If that's <u>too</u> fast, you can leave in a minute and a huff.

STAN LAUREL

A blizzard is the outside of a buzzard.

The first time I saw Jane Russell I wondered how she got her kneecaps up in her sweater.

Set in Sans Serif Bold.
Printed on Hallmark Eggshell Book paper.
Designed by Rosalyn Schanzer.